Getting To Know...

Nature's Children

RIVER OTTERS

Laima Dingwall

SCHOLASTIC INC.

New York Toronto London Auckland Sydney
Mexico City New Delhi Hong Kong Buenos Aires

Facts in Brief

Classification of the River Otter

Class: *Mammalia* (mammals)
Order: *Carnivora* (meat-eaters)
Family: *Mustelidae* (weasel family)
Genus: *Lontra*
Species: *Lontra canadensis*

World distribution. Exclusive to North America. Related species are found in South America, Europe, and Asia.

Habitat. Lakes, rivers, marshes, and ocean bays.

Distinctive physical characteristics. Thick, dark-brown fur; streamlined shape; short legs; webbed feet with furred soles.

Habits. Lives in family groups; playful; makes a variety of sounds; is comfortable on land as well as in water; most active at night; makes its home in the abandoned burrows of other animals.

Diet. Fish, crayfish, water insects, amphibians, birds, and small mammals.

Revised edition copyright © 1998 by Scholastic Inc.
Original material © 1985 Grolier Limited.
All rights reserved.

Published by Scholastic Inc.
90 Old Sherman Turnpike, Danbury, Connecticut 06816.

SCHOLASTIC and associated logos are trademarks of Scholastic Inc.

ISBN 0-7172-6695-8   Printed in the U.S.A.

Edited by: Elizabeth Grace Zuraw   *Photo Editor:* Nancy Norton
Photo Rights: Ivy Images   *Cover Design:* Niemand Design

Have you ever wondered . . .

what family the River Otter belongs to?	page 6
how big River Otters are?	page 6
if all River Otters live in rivers?	page 9
why a River Otter dives underwater?	page 14
how long a River Otter can stay underwater?	page 14
how fast a River Otter can swim?	page 14
what a River Otter uses its tail for?	page 17
why a River Otter is so comfortable in the water?	page 18
if a River Otter could outrun a man?	page 21
if the River Otter is a fussy eater?	page 22
what a River Otter uses its whiskers for?	page 22
why a River Otter must chew its food carefully?	page 25
when a River Otter sleeps?	page 26
if a River Otter makes a den?	page 26
what River Otters do in winter?	page 29
what kind of sounds a River Otter makes?	page 31
if River Otters like to play?	page 33
how a River Otter attracts a mate?	page 37
how a mother otter prepares her nursery?	page 38
what a newborn otter looks like?	page 38
what baby otters do all day?	page 40
how a mother otter teaches her babies to swim?	page 43
when young River Otters leave home?	page 46
Words To Know	page 47
Index	page 48

What furry little animal can be seen sliding on its belly down muddy hills at top speed, hiding pebbles on the bank of a stream, and juggling a chunk of food in its paws? If you guessed the River Otter, you're right.

This amusing creature has boundless energy and a seemingly endless supply of tricks. A whole family of otters will sometimes play hide-and-seek in the tall grass at the edge of a pond. In winter they might even try to slide up a snowy hill!

Learning about River Otters is almost as much fun as watching their antics. Read on to find out more about these amazing and playful little animals.

Expert swimmers, River Otters spend much time near or in water.

Meet the Relatives

The River Otter belongs to the weasel family. Its North American relatives include the mink, fisher, ermine, badger, wolverine, skunk, and marten.

Weasels come in all sizes. The Least Weasel is no bigger than a banana—about 8 inches (20 centimeters) long, while the Sea Otter can grow up to almost 5 feet (1.5 meters) and weigh as much as a ten-year-old child. In between is the River Otter.

The average male River Otter weighs about 18 pounds (8 kilograms) and measures a little more than 3 feet (1 meter) from the tip of its nose to the end of its tail. Female River Otters are slightly smaller.

No matter how big or small weasels are, they all have one thing in common. Their bodies produce a strong, sweet-smelling substance called *musk*. The River Otter, like other weasels, uses this musk at *mating* time, the time during which animals come together to produce young. An otter also uses the musk to mark its territory.

River Otter Country

River Otters are found throughout most of North America from northern Canada to the southern United States. Close relatives of the North American River Otter live throughout much of South America, Europe, and Asia.

Not all River Otters live in rivers. They make their homes in forests, on prairies, and on the northern tundra. Some even live on high mountains—so long as there is water nearby. A stream, a pond, a lake, a large marsh, or a coastal bay makes a good River Otter home.

The shaded area on this map shows where North American River Otters live.

The otter's streamlined body—agile and with a long tapered tail—is well suited for gliding through water.

Water Lovers

The River Otter is as comfortable and at home in water as you are on land. It's an excellent swimmer and uses a variety of "swimming strokes" to help it get around. It often glides lazily along on its stomach, pushing now and then with one foot. Occasionally it might flip onto its back or side and float in that position for a while.

At other times the River Otter moves in a snake-like way. Swimming on its belly, it dives and surfaces, dives and surfaces. First you see its head, then you see its tail, then its head, then its tail, and on and on.

Gentle, friendly, and playful, otters indulge in a remarkable array of water antics.

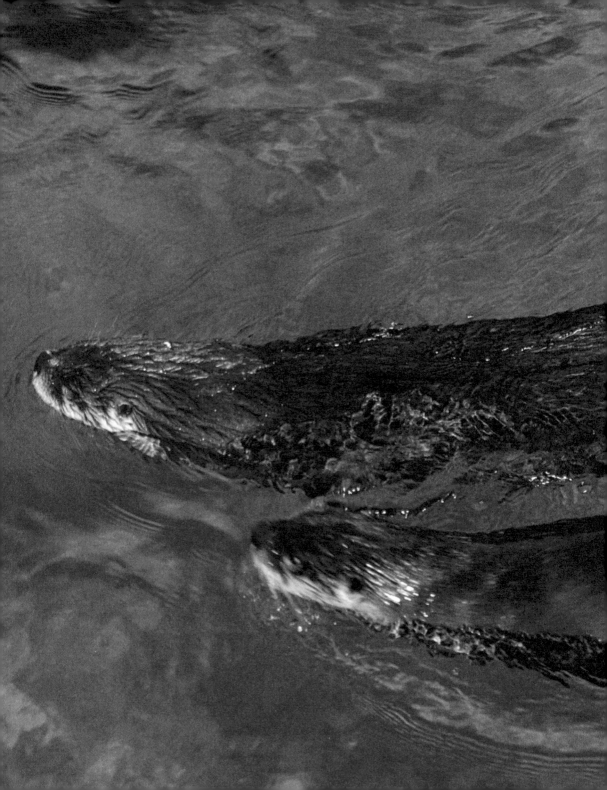

Follow the Leader

A family of otters sometimes plays "follow the leader." When the first otter dives underwater, the second in line comes to the surface. Meanwhile, the third otter dives while the last one surfaces. People have watched this display in amazement, thinking they've come upon a huge water serpent swishing through the water.

Opposite page: River Otters are highly social animals; they enjoy each other's company. Often, whole otter families play together.

River Otter underwater

Diving Champion

The River Otter dives underwater to find food, escape from enemies, get to its den, or just to play. It can stay under for four minutes or even longer before having to come up to the surface for a breath of air. How can the otter achieve this feat? It's able to slow down its heart rate. That way, the oxygen in its lungs lasts longer because it is used up more slowly.

When a River Otter is in a hurry underwater, it tucks its front feet close to its chest and its back feet close to its tail. Then it ripples its body up and down. Swimming underwater in this way, the otter can reach speeds of up to 7 miles (11 kilometers) per hour.

A River Otter can move through the water as fast as a canoeist.

Made for Water Living

The River Otter's body is well suited to all this swimming and diving. It has a sleek, streamlined shape to help it cut through the water quickly, and webbed feet to supply the paddle power. It holds its front feet close to its body and uses its big back feet to do most of the work.

When the River Otter is underwater, it sometimes needs to make sharp turns to keep up with fish it is trying to catch. That's when the otter uses its long thin tail as a rudder to help it change directions in a hurry.

A River Otter's hind foot

A long tail for steering and webbed feet for paddling make swimming easy work for a River Otter. This water-loving animal can stay under for four minutes or longer without coming up for air.

Keeping the Water Out

The River Otter has a sleek fur coat that not only is warm—it's waterproof, too! The otter's coat is actually two coats. An outer layer of long, stiff, *guard hairs* sheds water, while a layer of short *underfur* next to its body keeps in body heat.

The otter's nose and ears are waterproof, too. Its broad, black nose has its own built-in "nose plugs." These nose plugs are folds of skin that automatically cover the otter's nostrils when it dives underwater. Nor does water get into an otter's tiny round ears. It has built-in "ear plugs"—folds of skin that close over the inner ear to keep water out.

The River Otter's waterproof fur coat—as well as eyes and ears that shut automatically in water— enable the animal to be a vigorous swimmer.

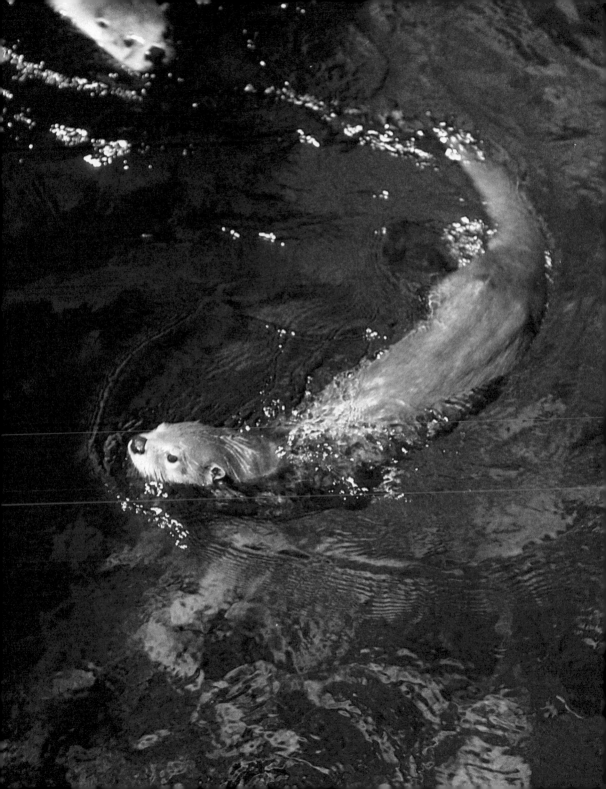

Land Sprinter

At first glance the River Otter looks clumsy and awkward on land. But even though its legs are short and stubby, they're powerful. The otter can gallop so fast that it can outrun a person over a short distance!

Usually, though, a River Otter pokes slowly along the banks of its home stream, river, or lake. It searches for food on land as well as in the water. The size of its feeding territory depends on the amount of food available. If food is scarce, its territory will be large. If food is plentiful, its territory will be smaller.

In winter when lakes and rivers freeze, otters sometimes travel overland in search of water that might still be flowing.

Big Appetite

The River Otter isn't fussy about its menu. It will eat small land animals such as muskrats, shrews, and young beavers, but most of its food comes from the water. A River Otter eats almost anything that swims or floats—fish, frogs, tadpoles, turtles, insects, and even ducks and other birds. Perhaps its favorite treats are the crayfish that live on the bottom of rivers and ponds.

To find crayfish and other bottom-dwellers, the otter dives all the way down and does a handstand on the floor of the river or pond. Then it pokes its nose into cracks, under rocks, between logs, or even into the mud. Its stiff bristly nose whiskers feel around in these nooks and crannies until they touch something. When this happens, nerves at the end of the whiskers send a "food!" message to the otter's brain. And the otter digs in.

The River Otter usually feeds just after dusk and then again before dawn.

Dainty Eater

You'll never see a River Otter gobbling down its food. When it has caught its dinner, it carefully carries the food to shore in its mouth or in its hand-like front paws. Then it takes small bites and chews carefully until the food is ground into tiny pieces. The otter has to do this because it has a narrow throat. If the food were swallowed in large chunks, the otter might choke.

Nibbling in this way, a full-grown otter eats about 3 pounds (1.5 kilograms) of food a day. That's about the same as 12 large hamburgers.

Fresh crab makes a tasty meal for a hungry River Otter.

A Cozy Home

The River Otter snoozes away most of the daylight hours in a *den,* or animal home, that has been abandoned by a beaver, muskrat, or other animal. Sometimes the den is between boulders along the shore or under the roots of fallen trees. Or it might be a comfortable spot in a thicket of marsh weeds.

As soon as the River Otter moves in, it starts to make improvements in its borrowed den. To make a cozy bed, the otter covers the floor with dried leaves, bark, or moss. Sometimes it hollows out a separate room to one side to use as a toilet. And the otter usually makes sure the den has two entrances—one underwater, the other on the ground. That way it can always dart out one entrance if an enemy comes in the other.

With an underwater entrance to its den, a River Otter can make a swift getaway if an intruder appears.

Life Under the Ice

For a long time scientists thought that River Otters sleep most of the winter. After all, the animals are seen only on very mild days. But River Otters are active all winter long. They just spend much of their time under the ice and snow. That's why they're so rarely seen.

When a river or pond freezes over, an otter can still fish for food under the ice. It comes up for air at breathing holes or breathes from pockets of air trapped under the ice. After a food excursion under the ice, the otter snuggles back into its cozy den.

When the otter travels above the ice, it often tunnels under the snow rather than walk through it. That's because its legs are so short. If it tried to walk through deep snow, it might get stuck.

Crossing ice is not a problem for the otter. Tufts of hair between its toes prevent it from slipping and keep its feet warm.

Even in winter, River Otters are at home in water. They fish under the ice on lakes and rivers.

River Otter Talk

If you walk near a pond or river and hear what sounds like a loud cough, you might be near a River Otter. When it is startled or frightened, the otter blows through its nose, making a snorting cough-like sound. This may be the otter's way of clearing its nostrils so that it can smell the air better in order to detect an enemy. Or it may be a way of telling other River Otters that danger is nearby. But some people think the snort is just a gasp of surprise.

There's no mistaking the sound of an angry River Otter, especially when it's face to face with an enemy, such as a lynx or other big cat. The otter opens its mouth wide to show all its strong teeth and it screams loudly. That tells the enemy, "Watch out or I'll bite!" Most animals take this warning seriously and retreat. If they don't, the otter will fight fiercely to defend itself.

The most common sounds a River Otter makes are a quiet chuckling "huh-huh-huh" sound and a soft bird-like "chirp-chirp-chirp." Those happy sounds are friendly otter-to-otter talk.

Opposite page: Chuckles, snorts, growls, chirps, and screams are some of the many sounds River Otters use to communicate with one another.

31

Fun and Games

It's impossible not to smile when you see a River Otter playing—it seems to be having so much fun!

The River Otter sometimes picks up pebbles, twigs, and shells and juggles them in its front paws. It might even balance a leaf on its nose. Or it might dive to the bottom of the pond and find a stone, then swim to the surface and float on its back, playing with the stone in its paws!

If the River Otter drops the stone, the game doesn't end. The otter just dives underwater again to find it. But on the way down it might be distracted by a fish and chase it for a while. Or it might simply chase its own tail around and around.

On land or in the water, few animals are as playful as the River Otter.

Family Antics

There are plenty of high jinks when a whole otter family gets together. They chase each other along the shore and into the water, rolling and tumbling together in a bunch. Or they slide down slippery mud-or grass-covered hills with front legs outstretched. The best hills for sliding are those near the river. Then the slide ends with a big splash.

River Otters like sliding so much that they'll even do it without a hill. On level ground they sometimes jump, jump, jump, s-l-i-d-e—three short jumps and one long slide.

Otter games don't stop when the snow falls. In fact, otters love nothing more than coasting down a snow-covered slope on their bellies. Sometimes a family of River Otters plays a rollicking wintertime version of hide-and-seek. One otter dives and tunnels under the deep snow, while another one jumps, rolls around, and pokes its nose into the snow, looking for its hidden playmate.

Whether on winter's snow or summer's mud, sliding down hills is a favorite pastime of the River Otter.

Mating Time

River Otters mate in late winter or early spring. At that time, the male makes musk in two *glands* under his tail. A gland is a part of an animal's body that makes and gives out a substance. The male leaves this musk smell around his *territory*, the area an animal lives in and defends from other animals of the same kind. The musk attracts females and warns other males to stay away. The female also leaves a musk smell to tell males that she is ready to mate.

Once a male River Otter finds a mate, the two otters play together. They chase one another in and out of the water, rolling and spinning as they go. After they have mated, the two otters go their separate ways. But although they don't live together, the male stays close to his mate's den.

The mating season of River Otters is March and April, but otter babies aren't born until the next spring.

River Otter Birthday

A mother otter turns her den into a nursery by lining it with plenty of dry leaves and soft grass. She usually has two or three babies in early spring, but sometimes there may be as many as five babies in her *litter*. A litter is the group of young animals born at the same time.

A newborn River Otter is tiny—about the size of a baby kitten. It weighs just over 4 ounces (100 grams) and measures barely 11 inches (28 centimeters) from the tip of its nose to the end of its tail. It's covered with short fuzzy fur and has short whiskers around its nose.

The newborn otter cannot see or hear. Its eyes and tiny round ears won't open until the baby is about 35 days old.

The whiskers of a River Otter, short and soft at birth, later grow stiff and long. They are used to search out prey and detect turbulence in water.

Life in the Den and Out

The baby otters spend their early weeks in the den. When they are not *nursing,* or drinking milk from their mother's body, they sleep in a heap beside her or tussle with each other in play-fights.

The River Otter mother leaves her babies only after dark, when she goes out for a short time to find food for herself. Even then she stays within hearing distance and hurries back to the den as soon as she can.

When the otter babies are about three months old, the mother lets them explore the world outside the den. By this time, the babies each weigh close to 3 pounds (1.5 kilograms).

The youngsters stagger out of the den and try out their legs. Running is a problem. Their legs are still weak and wobbly, and they tumble and fall over their own feet and over each other.

The normal life span of the River Otter is about eight or nine years.

Swimming Lessons

One of the first lessons the River Otter mother teaches her babies once they leave the den is how to swim. And that isn't easy. The tricky part is getting the babies into the water in the first place.

Sometimes the mother tries to coax her little ones into the water with gentle nose-nudging. Other times she swims out into the pond and chirps for her babies to follow. Usually the babies won't have any part of her urgings. They stand on the shore and refuse to get wet. Then the mother has no choice but to grab her youngsters one at a time by the scruff of the neck, tow them out into the middle of the pond, and then let go. At first the babies just bob around on the surface, but soon they learn to swim.

At first otter cubs don't willingly take to the water. They need to be coaxed into the river by their mother.

Fast Learners

In a few days the babies are so accustomed to the water that they follow their mother on her dives. They watch as she probes with her paws and whiskers on the bottom of the pond for crayfish and other treats. And they try to keep up when she swims after fish. The babies are fast learners and are soon catching their own dinners.

River Otter cubs stay with their mother for at least a year.

One Big Happy Family

By the fall, the young River Otters are about six months old and almost as big as their mother. Until this time they are raised by their mother alone. Then her mate joins her and both parents look after the young.

The River Otter family spends the fall and winter together. In the spring, when the young otters are almost one year old, they leave their parents. But they don't wander too far away. The young usually make their dens quite near their first home so there are always lots of otters nearby ready to play.

Words To Know

Den   Animal home.

Gland   A part of an animal's body that makes and gives out a substance.

Guard hairs   Long coarse hairs that make up the outer layer of the otter's coat.

Litter   The group of young animals born at the same time.

Marsh   A flat area of land covered with shallow water.

Mate   To come together to produce young.

Musk   A powerful smelling substance produced by the otter to mark its territory and attract a mate.

Nostrils   The openings that allow air into the nose.

Nurse   To drink milk from a mother's body.

Territory   Area that an animal or group of animals lives in and often defends from other animals of the same kind.

Tundra   A treeless region of the Arctic.

Underfur   Short, dense hair that traps body-warmed air next to an animal's skin.

Index

babies, 38, 40, 43, 45 46
belly, 5

coat, 18, 29
communication, 31

den, 14, 26, 29, 37, 38, 40, 46
description, 17
diet, 17, 22, 25, 45
distribution, 9
diving, 10, 13, 14, 17, 22

ears, 18

fall, 46
family, 13, 34, 46
feeding, 4, 21, 22, 25, 29, 40, 45
female, 6, 37, 38, 40, 43, 45, 46
fighting, 31, 37

growing up, 40, 43, 45, 46
guard hairs, 18

habitat, 5, 9, 45
home, 9, 10, 21, 26, 46
hunting, 17, 22

keeping warm, 18, 29

Least Weasel, 6
legs, 21
life span, 40
locomotion, 5, 10, 13, 14, 17, 21, 22, 29, 34

lungs, 14

male, 6, 37, 46
mating, 6, 37
mouth, 25, 31
musk, 6, 37

nose, 18, 22, 31

paws, 5, 14, 17, 25, 45
playing, 5, 13, 14, 33, 34, 37
protection, 26, 31, 40

relatives, 6

Sea Otter, 6
scent, 6, 37
size, 6
  of babies, 38
sleeping, 26, 29
spring, 37, 46
swimming, 10, 14, 17, 43

tail, 6, 14, 17, 37
teeth, 31
territory, 6, 21, 37
throat, 25
toes, 29
touch, 22

waterproofing, 18
whiskers, 22, 38, 45
winter, 29, 34, 37, 46

PHOTO CREDITS

Cover: Leonard Lee Rue III. **Interiors:** *Canada In Stock / Ivy Images:* Mario A. Madau, 4, 12; Jack Schachner, 16. /Bill Ivy, 7, 15. /Wayne Lankinen, 8, 30. /*Visuals Unlimited:* D. Cavagnaro, 11. /Barry Ranford, 19. /*Ivy Images:* Alan & Sandy Carey, 20, 23, 35, 42, 44; Robert McCaw, 27./Tim Fitzharris, 24. /J. D. Taylor, 28, 32. /*Valan Photos:* Thomas Kitchin, 36; M. J. Johnson, 39; J. A. Wilkinson, 41.

Getting To Know...

Nature's Children

RED FOX

Merebeth Switzer

SCHOLASTIC INC.

New York   Toronto   London   Auckland   Sydney
Mexico City   New Delhi   Hong Kong   Buenos Aires

Facts in Brief

Classification of the Red Fox

    Class: *Mammalia* (mammals)

    Order: *Carnivora* (meat-eaters)

    Family: *Canidae* (dog family)

    Genus: *Vulpes*

    Species: *Vulpes vulpes*

World distribution. Widely distributed throughout the Northern Hemisphere—in North America, Europe, Asia, and North Africa.

Habitat. Prefers semi-open country—mixed farmlands, forest clearings, tundra.

Distinctive physical characteristics. Coat usually reddish brown with white patches on the underparts; bushy, white-tipped tail; furred foot pads.

Habits. Active mainly at night; skilled at eluding enemies; often mates for life; both parents care for young.

Diet. Mice, rabbits and other small mammals, birds, insects, eggs, and to a lesser extent, vegetable matter.

Published by Scholastic Inc.
90 Old Sherman Turnpike, Danbury, Connecticut 06816.

SCHOLASTIC and associated logos are trademarks of Scholastic Inc.

ISBN 0-7172-6695-8   Printed in the U.S.A.

Edited by: Elizabeth Grace Zuraw   *Photo Editor:* Nancy Norton
Photo Rights: Ivy Images   *Cover Design*: Niemand Design

Have you ever wondered . . .

what Red Fox cubs learn from playing? page 6

if the Red Fox has many relatives? page 8

where Red Foxes can be found? page 8

why Red Foxes like to be near settled areas? page 11

if all Red Foxes are red? page 15

where a Red Fox sleeps? page 16

how a Red Fox keeps its feet warm in cold weather? page 16

how a Red Fox escapes its enemies? page 21

what a Red Fox eats? page 22

how Red Foxes help farmers? page 25

how a Red Fox hunts? page 26

how to tell a Red Fox's age? page 29

how long Red Foxes usually live? page 29

how Red Foxes communicate with each other? page 31

if Red Foxes ever fight with each other? page 33

how a Red Fox chooses a mate? page 33

how a Red Fox mother prepares for her babies? page 34

how many babies a mother Red Fox has? page 39

what newborn Red Foxes look like? page 39

how the Red Fox father helps look after the family? page 39

when Red Fox cubs first leave the den? page 40

how a Red Fox mother feeds her cubs? page 42

how Red Fox cubs learn to hunt? page 44

when Red Fox cubs leave home? page 46

Words To Know page 47

Index page 48

Think of a story you know that has a fox in it. What is the fox like? In the stories about Brer Rabbit, Brer Fox plays tricks on Brer Rabbit all the time. The fox in *Pinocchio* is forever getting children into all sorts of trouble. And in Aesop's fables, a crow gets a good taste of a fox's craftiness.

Sneaky, sly troublemakers—that's how foxes appear in many stories. But real foxes don't deserve this bad reputation. They may seem to be sneaky or sly at times, but they are only being clever in order to hunt for food and escape enemies.

Read on to find out more about one very smart fox, the Red Fox.

Shy, smart, alert, and clever are but a few ways to describe the handsome Red Fox.

Meet a Red Fox Cub

Red Fox cubs love to play, and they make toys out of just about anything. A fox mother brings home special treats for her growing cubs. Bones, feathers, and sticks become playthings for the youngsters to chew, tug, and fight over.

Red Fox cubs, sometimes also called *pups*, are not big, but they make loud squeals. These noisy balls of fur have not yet learned that a good hunter is a quiet hunter. But their play teaches them other lessons, such as how to grab and hold on to *prey*, animals hunted by other animals for food. The skills fox cubs learn in play will come in handy when the young foxes must hunt for themselves.

Usually four to ten cubs are born in a litter, *the group of animals born together.*

Red Fox

Coyote

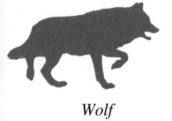

Wolf

A Cousin for Rover

You might not be surprised to learn that the Red Fox has several fox relatives—the Arctic Fox, the Gray Fox, the African Fennec Fox, the Kit Fox, and the Swift Fox. But would you have guessed that the Red Fox is also related to the Timber Wolf, the coyote, and even to dogs?

There are more Red Foxes than any other type of fox. Red Foxes live throughout most of North America and are also found across all of Europe, most of Asia, and even in parts of northern Africa, India, and Japan.

Where Red Foxes live in North America

A Surprise for Settlers

When the pioneers first arrived in North America, they cleared the land for farms. To get away from the settlers, many wild animals moved deeper into the wilderness—but not the Red Fox. This clever animal found that the open fields and pastures and the crops of the new farms made a good hunting ground. Mice and other small animals could be readily caught for food, and empty woodchuck dens made a good home for raising a family. Then in winter, farm woodlots sheltered the Red Fox from chilly winds and snow. The early pioneers had created a perfect home for foxes! Soon there were many more Red Foxes than there had been before the settlers arrived.

Though most active at night, the Red Fox is sometimes seen in early morning or late afternoon.

Sizing Up the Fox

The Red Fox weighs about as much as a small dog, and it's not much taller than a Bassett Hound. Its beautiful bushy tail is almost as long as the rest of its body.

The male fox, or *dog*, is usually larger than the female, or *vixen*. And Red Foxes are larger in northern areas than they are in southern regions. In the north, the extra weight protects the fox from the cold because it keeps the body from losing heat too quickly. The thick winter fur of a northern fox makes it look bigger, too.

One of the first things you notice about a Red Fox is its long and very bushy tail, often tipped with white fur.

A Fancy Dresser

The Red Fox is a very elegant looking animal. It even has black fur on its legs, making it look as if it's wearing handsome black stockings.

Are Red Foxes red? Not always. Just as you and your friends have different colors of hair—blond or red or brown or black—so, too, do Red Foxes. In fact, sometimes young foxes in the same family have different colors of fur.

The Red Fox's fur most often is a reddish-brown, but it may also be a beautiful silver or black. Many Red Foxes have buff or white patches on their body—on the tip of their tail, chest, belly, or even on their lips. Some Red Foxes even have a dark-brown or black cross pattern on their shoulders and down the middle of their back. These are called *cross foxes*.

When the hot weather of summer is over, the Red Fox starts to grow its thick winter coat. That way it will stay toasty warm by the time the first snow falls.

Snoozing in a Snowbank

How would you keep warm if you had to sleep outdoors all winter long? A good sleeping bag and blankets would help. But a fox doesn't have blankets to keep it warm. Instead it has a double thick fur coat. An outer layer of long, smooth *guard hairs* cover the warm, thick *underfur* of the fox's coat. The guard hairs serve as a waterproof windbreaker, keeping out water and cold wind. The woolly underfur is like cozy underwear next to the fox's body, keeping it warm. On cold days, the fox looks for a place that is out of the wind, such as a hollow at the edge of a snowbank. There it curls up into a tight ball and folds its furry tail over its nose and paws. The snow acts as a kind of blanket, helping to keep the fox warm.

You might not find it very cozy to be curled up in the snow, but with its thick fur coat, the Red Fox finds it quite comfortable.

The Tracks of a Traveler

The Red Fox hunts for food all winter long. Every night it may travel for several hours searching for a meal. If a fox were to get cold feet in winter, it wouldn't be able to hunt for the food it needs to live. To keep its feet warm, a fox has fur between its toes. This fur also gives the fox a better grip when running across slippery ice or snow. If you ever spot fox tracks, look closely. You may be able to see the marks left by these hairs.

Trotting along a cold wintry terrain is no problem for a fox. Its furry footpads keep its feet warm.

Outfoxed by a Fox

Some animals climb trees for safety, others hide in dens. But not the Red Fox. It has other tricks to help it escape enemies.

A Red Fox is quite skillful in leading its enemy on a merry chase. Through a manure pile, along a carefully balanced log, into a patch of raspberries—a fox will venture anywhere. And each game of chase can be quite different— perhaps a short swim in a pond or a mad dash across a highway. If you were a bear trying to catch a fox, would you follow it through such a challenging obstacle course—or would you just give up?

The Red Fox is famous for "outfoxing" all who try to catch it, even humans. And it's because the Red Fox is so smart at getting away that it is known for being cunning, sly, and crafty.

For avoiding enemies, the Red Fox has more than cleverness on its side. It also has speed. It can run as fast as 6 miles (10 kilometers) an hour.

Fox tracks

21

A Meal Everywhere

The Red Fox eats almost anything. This is one of the reasons it has survived so well. The fox likes rabbits, voles, mice, and other small rodents best, but it also eats insects, snails, eggs, and other foods that it finds on its travels. If a fox is lucky enough to kill a large animal, it may bury the part it doesn't eat right away and save it for a meal later on. If meat is scarce, foxes will also eat fruits such as blueberries and apples.

A sharp sense of smell enables the Red Fox to sniff out insects even when they are hidden in the bark of an old storm-damaged tree.

Friend or Enemy?

Foxes sometimes hunt farm animals such as chickens and turkeys, and they've been known to steal eggs. This behavior has given them a bad reputation among farmers. But foxes also help farmers by catching mice and other small animals that eat crops and ruin stored grain.

In some places where foxes have been removed, the mouse population increased so much that farmers have had to bring in other foxes to help control the rodents.

Mice, rabbits, birds, and other small animals, as well as insects and fruits, are on a fox's menu—along with an occasional raid on a farmer's hen house.

Looking for Clues

The fox uses its keen nose, sharp eyes, and good ears to help it hunt. The movement of a rabbit hiding in the tall grass, the squeak of a mouse as it scurries along under the snow, or the smell of a bird hidden in the bush are all clues that lead a fox to its next meal.

To catch a mouse, a Red Fox pounces and traps it between its front paws, just like a cat. Also like a cat, a fox may sit without moving and wait for a long time before jumping on its prey. Sometimes a fox may quietly lie in wait near a woodchuck's burrow and pounce on the unsuspecting animal as it leaves its home.

When hunting during the day, Red Foxes use their sharp vision as well as their excellent hearing and sense of smell. This fox feasted on a bird for lunch—only a feather is left hanging from the fox's mouth.

Teeth Like a Tree?

The fox's teeth stay hard and sharp because a new layer of *enamel*, the hard outer covering of teeth, grows each year. Have you ever counted the rings on a tree stump to see how old the tree was? In the same way, scientists can tell how old a fox is by looking at one of its teeth. If you cut a fox's tooth in half, you can see a ring for each new layer of enamel. You can tell how old a fox is by counting the enamel rings on the tooth.

By studying fox teeth in this way, scientists have found that many foxes die from disease or are killed when they are young by *predators*, animals that hunt other animals for food. Those foxes that learn to hunt and defend themselves will often live to 12 years of age or older.

Red Fox tooth

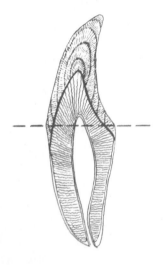

Cross-section showing enamel "age" rings

The Red Fox, a carnivore, *has 42 teeth.*
A carnivore is an animal that eats flesh.

Short, yapping barks are one way that foxes communicate with each other.

Keep Out

Foxes "talk" to other foxes by using different barks, growls, and yelps, just as dogs do. Every now and then a fox might even howl.

But foxes don't always bark their messages. Sometimes they send silent messages. How? The male fox urinates against trees and other upright objects. These "scent posts" tell other foxes, "This territory is already taken." A *territory* is the area that an animal lives in and defends from other animals.

If an intruder ignores the message, it may be in for a fight. Sometimes both foxes stand on their hind legs, hitting each other with their front paws and biting at each other's muzzle.

To avoid being hurt, the weaker fox usually admits defeat quickly. Crouching close to the ground with its ears flat against its head, it wails a cry that says, "You're the boss."

The victorious fox may then show off. It fluffs up its fur, making itself look much bigger than it really is, and it struts stiff-legged over to a scent post to mark it. This tells the loser it's time for a quick exit.

Choosing a Mate

During *mating season*, the time of year during which animals come together to produce young, several male foxes may compete to win a mate. They strut back and forth, trying to impress the female. Sometimes two males may even fight for her. In these fights the strongest animal wins. This means that the babies it fathers are likely to be strong, too.

Often the dog fox and vixen stay together for all their lives. Sometimes Red Foxes live in a small group, with the dog fox having more than one mate. But usually one vixen will be *dominant*, of a higher rank than the other vixens.

The fox pair has a hunting territory that is about the size of 70 city blocks. The pair will share this territory with another dog fox only if there are no babies to protect. Young foxes are too precious to trust around a stranger.

The Red Fox thrives in open grass and farmland where there is plenty of food.

Borrowing a Burrow

When it's almost time for their cubs to be born, the Red Fox parents look for a good place to make a *den*, or animal home.

Foxes are not great den diggers. They prefer to borrow an unused den abandoned by another animal, such as a woodchuck or badger. Sometimes, however, the mother fox must make do with a small cave, a hollow tree trunk, or a thicket of bushes for a nursery. Although she seldom digs her own den, she may make an existing burrow bigger by digging out rooms and adding entrances. Often one entrance faces south to help keep the den warm. Usually the den has a small clearing at the main entrance. Later this cleared area will serve as a playground for the young fox cubs.

The foxes will use the same den year after year. They often make more than one den so that the young can be moved quickly if there is danger.

Cutaway of a Red Fox den

Father Brings Home the Food

While the female fox finishes preparing the nursery den by lining it with leaves and grass, the male hunts and brings food for her. The vixen does not let him into the den, so he leaves the food outside the entrance. Any food she does not eat, she saves to eat later, when the babies are born.

Though often on the move, sometimes a fox likes just resting quietly in the clearing outside its den, enjoying the warmth of the sun.

Happy Birthday, Cubs!

Not long after the vixen settles into her den, the cubs are born. There are anywhere from four to ten cubs in a litter. The babies are helpless bundles of woolly brown fur, and they cannot see or hear for the first ten days. They are content to sleep and *nurse*, or drink the rich milk in their mother's body.

During this time the dog fox brings food for the mother. He has not yet seen the cubs, but it won't be long before it's time for both the mother and father to share the hunting and the care of the youngsters.

As soon as the newborns' eyes open—about nine days after birth—and the cubs start to crawl, the father is allowed into the den. While he "baby-sits," the mother goes off to hunt. But the mother fox never goes too far away. Her babies are growing quickly, and they need to drink her milk often during the first weeks of their life.

Opposite page: With keenly alert ears, even young fox cubs can hear a little mouse squeaking in the grass up to 100 feet (30 meters) away.

Hello, World!

By the time they are one month old, the cubs are strong enough to leave the den for the first time. As they poke their heads into the sunshine, they blink furiously. The new world outside is awfully bright after the dimness of the den.

The mother fox keeps her babies in the small clearing in front of the den's main entrance. Like many other youngsters, the cubs are shy in unfamiliar places. If a leaf blows across the dirt, they go scurrying back inside the den. But in a matter of days, the lively cubs will be comfortable in their new outdoor surroundings. There they'll wrestle and pounce on one another, playful and fearless as kittens.

When fox parents return home safely after a hunt, they're always a welcome sight to their cubs.

Mini Meat-eaters

At about the time the cubs begin to leave the den, they're also ready to eat their first meat. Like most babies, they start with baby food. Their tiny teeth and young stomachs are not yet quite ready for big chunks of meat. To make this "baby food," the mother fox chews and swallows the meat. When her cubs cry for food, she brings up the food. For the cubs, eating is easier when food is first chewed and half-digested in this way. And it's also easier for the mother fox to carry food back to the den in her stomach rather than in her teeth.

At birth, Red Fox cubs weigh about 4 ounces (110 grams). By the time they become adults, males will weigh about 12 pounds (5.9 kilograms). Females will weigh a little less.

Learning Through Play

With each day, the cubs' play becomes rougher. They're becoming braver and more daring in the world around them. A young fox learns how to hunt as it plays at fighting, chasing, and stalking its brothers and sisters.

To practice hunting skills, the cubs pounce on butterflies and beetles. The mice and voles put at their feet by the fox parents become toys to fight over and toss and tear before eating. In this way the young foxes also learn about the types of food to hunt.

The cubs grow up quickly. By early fall they are nearly three-quarters the size of their parents, and their adult coat of thick fur has grown in. They are also becoming skilled hunters.

Cubs spend a lot of time play-fighting and pouncing on one another, but such play has a serious side. It prepares the cubs for hunting prey.

Family Good-byes

Now it is time for all the foxes in the family to go their own way. The mother and father leave first, one after the other. They will not meet again until mating season the next spring. Then the young foxes set off on their own.

If the winter hunting is good, the brother and sister cubs may not go far from each other. But usually each young fox goes off alone, often traveling more than 30 miles (50 kilometers) to find its own hunting territory.

The young Red Fox will not be alone for long. In January, it will be time for it to look for a mate and to start a family of its own.

Words To Know

Burrow A hole in the ground dug by an animal to be used as a home.

Carnivore An animal that eats flesh.

Cross fox A Red Fox that has a black fur cross pattern down the middle of its back.

Cubs Young foxes, also called pups.

Den Animal home.

Dog The name for the male fox.

Dominant Of a higher rank.

Enamel The hard outer covering of teeth.

Guard hairs Long coarse hairs that make up the outer layer of a fox's coat.

Litter Young animals born together.

Mating season The time of year during which animals come together to produce young.

Nurse To drink the mother's milk.

Predator An animal that hunts other animals for food.

Prey An animal hunted by other animals for food.

Territory Area that an animal or group of animals lives in and often defends from other animals of the same kind.

Underfur Short, dense hair that traps body-warmed air next to an animal's skin.

Vixen The name of a female fox.

Index

African Fennec Fox, 8
Arctic Fox, 8

baby: *see* cubs
burrow: *see* den

coat, 12, 15, 16, 44
climbing, 21
color, 15
communication, 31, 39
cross fox, 15
cubs, 6, 15, 34, 39, 40, 42, 44, 46

den, 11, 33, 34, 37, 40,
diet, 22, 25,
digging, 34
distribution, 8
dog, 12, 33, 37, 39, 44, 46

eating habits
  of adults, 22
  of cubs, 39, 42
enemies, 5, 21, 34

feet, 18
female: *see* vixen
fighting, 31

Gray Fox, 8
guard hairs, 16

habitat, 11
help to farmers, 25

hunting, 5, 6, 11, 18, 25, 26, 37,
  39, 44
hunting tactics, 26

Kit Fox, 8

life span, 29

male: *see* dog
markings, 15
mating season, 33, 46

night, 18

playing, 6, 34, 40, 44

relatives, 8

scent posts, 26, 40
size, 12, 42, 44
spring, 46
Swift Fox, 8
swimming, 21

tail, 12, 15, 16
talking, 6, 31
teeth, 29
territory, 31, 33, 46
tracks, 18, 21

underfur, 16

vixen, 12, 33, 37, 39, 40, 42, 46

waterproofing, 16
winter, 11, 15, 16, 18, 46

PHOTO CREDITS
Cover: Robert McCaw, *Ivy Images*. **Interiors:** Bill Ivy, 4, 32. /*Ivy Images:* Robert McCaw, 7, 14, 23, 27, 30; Norman Lightfoot, 19; Don Johnston, 28. /*Canada In Stock / Ivy Images:* Gilles Daigle, 9; Ron Erwin, 36-37; Brian M. Wolitski, 38. /*Eco-Art Productions:* Norman Lightfoot, 10, 20, 24. /Wayne Lankinen, 13, 41. /*Valan Photos:* Wayne Lankinen, 17. /*Tom Stack & Associates:* Eric A. Soder, 43. /*Hot Shots / Ivy Images:* Jeff Simpson, 45.